1. What does this booklet offer?

The
orga
forn
be i
achievement:

Tthis booklet is based on classroom research undertaken by the assessment team at King's College London. The background to this research is found in section 2 below. Many of the findings of the research will seem familiar to teachers of English who understand well the benefits of classroom dialogue as an aid to learning or the power of peer and self-assessment. What this booklet offers is an opportunity to reconsider these approaches in the light of the research findings on formative assessment and to use them more rigorously and consistently as a means of helping pupils to progress.

In an educational climate that pressurises teachers to 'deliver the goods', and where it has been suggested that English teachers rewrite their curriculum to cover the demands of the National Literacy Framework, the actual needs of the pupils can all too easily be overlooked and the time for teachers to reflect on their practice diminished.

This booklet will begin, therefore, by re-examining the aims of the teaching of English, and the principles of learning that underpin formative assessment, before going on to consider how these might be applied in the classroom.

- classroom talk – including the activities to promote talk and the role of questioning;
- feedback;
- sharing learning intentions and success criteria with the learner; and
- peer and self-assessment.

While each one will be considered discretely, all of them overlap. How can pupils assess themselves or their peers without understanding the criteria? How can feedback be meaningful unless the task is appropriate? More importantly, each of these aspects is underpinned by the organising premise that it is the relationship between the teacher and the pupil that is crucial in developing a formative classroom. As Black and Wiliam observe, it is 'the quality of the interaction [between pupil and teacher] which is at the heart of pedagogy' (1998a: 16). What we offer, therefore, is neither a prescribed formula nor a 'How to' manual, but rather a 'rough guide' or *aide-mémoire* to formative practice. This is because formative assessment is considerably more than the sum of a series of handy tips and techniques; it is about creating a learning culture within the classroom that enables the pupil to become an independent and effective learner.

2. Background

A review of research published in 1998, both as a full article and in summary form as a short booklet for teachers (Black and Wiliam 1998a, 1998b), is the origin of the findings on which this booklet is based. That work established that there is strong evidence that formative assessment can raise standards of pupil achievement, but that the requisite assessment practices were not implemented in most classrooms. This led the group at King's College London to explore the potential for practical improvement by collaborating with a group of teachers willing to take on the risks and extra work involved, with support from their schools and LEAs. Through collaboration with Medway and Oxfordshire, we were able to recruit six secondary schools, spanning a range of catchment backgrounds. At the outset, 12 science and 12 mathematics teachers were involved. Twelve English teachers joined in the work a year later.

The first outcome, which took over two years to achieve, was that almost all of the teachers were positive about its effects for them, and that there were significant gains in test performance for the classes involved (Wiliam et al. 2004). On the basis of observations and records of visits to classrooms by our team, records of meetings of the whole group of teachers, interviews with and writing by the teachers themselves, and discussions with pupil groups, we were able to summarise the findings in a second short booklet for teachers (Black et al. 2002) and to report them at length both in a book (Black et al. 2003) and in many papers in professional and research journals.

Following that project, members of the King's team have made numerous contributions to teachers' conferences and to school and LEA inservice training. We have also been helping in developments on a larger scale, notably with the Scottish Education Department and with the States of Jersey. The development of formative assessment has also been made a significant component of the DfES initiative for Key Stage 3, work to which the King's team are also making direct contributions.

Throughout this work, we have always been aware that formative assessment has both *generic* features, i.e. features that will apply to learning across all stages and all school subjects, and features which are *specific* to primary teachers and to individual subjects. In this booklet we focus on the needs and opportunities that are most relevant to secondary school teachers of English.

3. Aims of English teaching

'English' is really an umbrella term for a number of different disciplines, and therein lies part of the difficulty in defining the aims of the subject in a way that will satisfy all those who teach it; that and the fact that an opinion on how English should be taught has always been a convenient cover for a more general view of life and society. A writer in the *Daily Telegraph* suggested that, 'Without the insights of grammar, civilisation collapses' (Howse 2004). A rather different perspective is suggested by an advocate of critical literacy who wants pupils to ask 'how language might be put to different more equitable uses, and how texts might be (re)created to tell a different story of other possibilities in a more just world (Morgan and Wyatt-Smith 2000: 127).

Moreover, the teaching of English has, in the last fifteen or so years, seen an unprecedented number of policy interventions, both to the curriculum and to how it is assessed. Since 1988 there has been a commission into the teaching of language (DES and WO [Kingman Report] 1990a); an unpublished but widely distributed set of materials, *Language in the National Curriculum*, arising from that report (Carter 1992); three versions of the National Curriculum (DES and WO 1990b; DFE and WO 1995; DfEE/QCA 2000); and the literacy framework for both the primary and the secondary phases (DfEE 1998; DfEE

2001). In the same period, national testing for seven-, eleven- and fourteen-year-olds has been introduced, as well as four sets of changes to the way in which GCSE English has been examined and a major overhaul of the A-level syllabus, including assessment at AS-level. All of these have had an impact on the way in which English is taught and experienced by pupils.

While people may nuance the subject of English in particular ways, many, if not most, agree that English is about the art of language. This aesthetic dimension distinguishes English from both literacy and communication studies in that it emphasises the imaginative and creative scope of the subject; the possibility of forming ideas into words (though the importance of technical acumen and an ability to convey meaning are, of course, also essential elements of English).

This does, however, make any discussion of progression difficult in that it is hard to be precise about what the trajectory of the development of the imagination might be, or why one way of expressing something works better than another. It is sometimes possible to offer a retrospective explanatory analysis when comparing two pieces of work but the complexity of any given piece of writing means it is hard to itemise or predict in advance the features that might make it good except in the most general of terms.

Any attempt at being more precise runs the risk of missing an essential ingredient. (For a fuller discussion of this see Marshall 2004a and b.) Crucial to English learning and teaching, then, is the development of judgement. In this way assessment, which is, after all, a type of judgement, lies at the heart of the subject discipline.

4. Principles of learning

The first and most important principle is that the pupil is engaged in the process. Black and Wiliam defined formative assessment as:

all those activities undertaken by teachers, *and by their students in assessing themselves,* which provide information to be used as feedback to modify the teaching and learning activities in which they are engaged. *Such assessment becomes 'formative assessment' when the evidence is actually used to adapt the teaching work to meet the needs.* (Black and Wiliam 1998b: 2, original emphasis)

Crucially, therefore, formative assessment cannot be done to the pupils but must be done *with* them. The aim is to enable pupils to become independent learners. For this to be effective, pupils need time and opportunity to explore and discuss their ideas in order for the teacher to listen to where they are going and to intervene appropriately.

This leads to a second principle, which is that talk is an aid to learning. Again this principle once underpinned much that was deemed good practice in English teaching (see, for example, the work of Barnes *et al.* 1972 and the publications of the National Oracy and National Writing Projects). A more recent advocate of such practice is Roy Corden in his book *Literacy and Learning through Talk* (2000). Corden's research draws on the work of Vygotsky and Bruner, who suggested that in order to develop more mature capabilities in language pupils needed to interact with those who have already developed those capabilities. The interaction with peers and teachers provides a 'scaffolding' for the learner through which the learner develops the capabilities him/herself.

Practically, this involves English teachers in carefully devising and creating tasks that maximise opportunities for pupils to think through and develop their ideas as an aid to understanding and writing. The richer the task, the more meaningful the teachers' feedback. For within this model of teaching and learning the most frequent form of feedback will be oral – characteristically, based on the research evidence of the King's, Medway and Oxfordshire Formative Assessment Group (KMOFAP), a follow-up question that prompts further thinking.

Finally, in English, pupils need to learn to develop judgement about the quality of work they and others produce. Royce Sadler (1989) has described this as 'guild knowledge'. Significantly, he suggests that simply providing lists of criteria for what makes for a good piece of writing or performance is insufficient to help pupils progress because:

- the whole is always more than the sum of its constituent parts;
- the interrelationship between all the constituent components is always too complex to be itemised meaningfully; and
- the diversity of potential outcomes makes the use of criteria too restrictive to be helpful in suggesting progression.

Instead, he argues, pupils need to be apprenticed into the guild through the assessment process. Elsewhere, one of us has suggested that English teachers develop – principally through assessing pupils' work and through attending standardising meetings – a shared construct of what a particular grade looks like (Wiliam 2000). Observations of these standardisation meetings illustrate the point (see Marshall 2000). In these meetings the use of criteria is always subordinate to the teacher's overall impression of the quality of the candidates' work. In one exchange, for example, a moderator exhorts teachers not to take a tick box approach to criteria because a particular candidate 'screams D at me' (ibid.). What is vital to the process is the way in which the teachers learn to interpret the evidence.

Peer and self-assessment enables pupils to begin the development of a similar understanding of the construct that the community of teachers of English already shares. Discussion about their own writing and those of others enables them to gain insight into what is involved in good writing and thus apprentices pupils into the guild. In so doing it extends the range and scope of their repertoire. This is a very different process from pupils being encouraged to follow predetermined rules of a genre or grammatical patterns. Instead it starts with the premise that the use of language is about having something to say, about creating meaning, and that the process of writing is about moulding ideas and experience into communicable form. In this way the relationship between reading and writing becomes vital (for a fuller discussion of this principle see Barrs 2003 and Marshall 2004a).

5. Classroom talk

It is important to note, before we continue, that there is no substitute for the teacher actually being interested in what the pupils have to say.

At the heart of all true dialogue lies the relationship between the participants. Any practical advice on how to encourage longer responses on the part of pupils, or ways of managing whole-class discussion, has to be understood in this context. There are, however, ways in which teachers, who are interested in what their pupils have to say, can facilitate greater participation from all pupils.

Based on our research, most English lessons typically follow a pattern, which involves:

- whole-class teacher–pupil dialogue at the start of the lesson as the task is initiated;
- some form of pupil activity which involves talk for part of the lesson;
- followed by feedback on this activity directed by the teacher.

This latter activity may or may not be followed by further pupil activity.

Within this very general format, classroom talk takes a variety of forms but can broadly be divided into two different types:

- dialogue between the teacher and pupils;
- discussion between pupils.

As we have seen, talk is vital in enabling pupils to develop their ideas and thinking and so make progress. The two types of classroom talk outlined above also give teachers a means of gaining insight into pupils' thinking and provide a chance to develop further their ideas through the feedback they give the pupils. 'All such work involves some degree of feedback between those taught and the teacher, and this is entailed in the quality of the interaction which is at the heart of pedagogy' (Black and Wiliam 1998b:16).

This is only possible, however, if classroom discussion develops beyond a series of rapid-fire closed questions – which seem pacey but often only include a few pupils and allow little time for reflection – towards an atmosphere where the activities are so scaffolded that they offer real opportunities for thinking. The key to ensuring progression, then, lies in the nature of the task, the quality of the intervention made by the teacher and the relationship between these two elements.

A helpful way of understanding the dynamic of the classroom and the constraints and affordances it offers for feedback and pupil progression is Perrenoud's (1998) concept of the regulation of learning. He describes different types of classrooms. In some of these, those he calls traditional, learning is highly regulated and prescribed. The scope of the activities is tightly defined. The outcomes of the learning are largely content driven and predetermined, and pupils complete a series of narrow activities that are designed to cover the prescribed learning objectives. There is little opportunity for the pupils to own their own learning and the only information it gives teachers is a deficit model of what they cannot do according to the narrowly defined terms of reference.

In another type of classroom, which we might call discursive or negotiated, the tasks are more open-ended. Then the scope for pupils to govern their own thinking is greater and the possibility for the teachers to feed back meaningfully is enhanced; for in this type of classroom, 'regulation does not include setting up activities suggested to, or imposed on, the pupils but their adjustment once they have been initiated' (Perrenoud 1998: 88).

So what might this look like in practice? If we examine the two lessons below we can see the way in which the type of activities devised by teachers, and undertaken by pupils, contributes to the creation of a 'traditional' or 'discursive' classroom, and in so doing, the way in which the activities determine the quality of talk that takes place as an aid to progression. The two types of classroom talk identified at the start of the section are a helpful way of understanding this.

A Traditonal	B Discursive
Yr 8 Lesson A – Pre-20th C short story	*Yr 8 Lesson B – Pre-20th C poem*
• Teacher models criteria by sampling examples from the text she wishes them to correct.	• Class draw up list of criteria guided by teacher.
• Pupils correct text.	• Teacher and LSA perform poem.
• Teacher checks answers with whole class.	• Pupils asked to critique performance.
• Pupils correct each other's work.	• Pupils rehearse performance.
	• Pupils peer-assess poems based on criteria.
	• Pupils perform poems based on criteria.

Dialogue between the teacher and pupils

Like many English lessons, the two lessons were designed to engage pupils both with the content of the subject – in this case pre-twentieth-century texts – and with their own performance in English through a related, creative task. In one, this took the form of a piece of writing; in the other, speaking and listening. In lesson A the pupils had written a letter as one of the characters for homework and were using this lesson as an opportunity to improve their work. In lesson B the pupils had read the poem in the previous lesson and were now being asked to perform a section of it in the lesson in question.

The focus of the first activity in lesson A was on technical accuracy. The teacher handed out a text in which there were several deliberate errors of a technical variety – principally spelling and punctuation – which she wanted them to correct. All the interchanges revolved around notions of correctness and there was little scope for anything other than closed questions that had a right answer. Moreover, it was the teacher who set the agenda in terms of what the pupils would be looking for in the piece of work they were to mark.

The second activity in lesson A again centred on the teacher checking whether or not the pupils had found the errors in the text. The feedback involved pupils volunteering where they had found a mistake, and then the correction they had made. Occasionally they missed something in the text and the teacher would go back until a pupil identified the missing error and corrected it. Similarly, on the small number of occasions when a pupil got the answer wrong, the teacher would pause and wait for another pupil to volunteer the right answer. In this exchange the teacher adjudicated questions of correctness and there was no opportunity for the pupils to extend the narrowly defined scope of the task.

In contrast, the initial pupil–teacher dialogue in lesson B concentrated attention on issues to do with quality. The exchanges were more open and provided more opportunity for the pupils' answers to be probed and so extend their understanding of what makes for a good performance. The pupils were, to an extent, setting the agenda, in that they were being asked to propose success criteria, and thus being drawn into questions of quality and judgement – arguably core activities in English.

Yet the teacher did not abdicate responsibility; she subtly guided their responses. Through interaction, she also developed the pupils' critical vocabulary as the pupils' contributions were negotiated with the teacher, who, through exchange, refined them. Interestingly, the Japanese have a useful term for describing such a process – *neriage*, which means polishing. In Japan, recapitulating the contributions made by pupils is an important part of teachers' classroom practice. It provides an opportunity for teachers to synthesise the contributions made by different pupils, to interject specific vocabulary and to refine or re-contextualise ideas. An example of this refining process in lesson B would be the following exchange:

P: You could speed it up and slow it down.
T: Yes – pace, that's very important in reading [teacher then writes the word 'pace' on the board].

In the second series of interchanges in lesson B between pupils and teacher, as with the previous dialogue, it is the pupils' ideas that are being sought, the teacher attempting to understand. In this way, the locus of control shifts from the teacher to the pupil, although as Perrenoud suggests, it is the teacher who regulates the learning environment by adjusting the activity 'once it has been initiated'.

The reading by the learning support assistant (LSA) was accompanied by a freeze-frame by the teacher (the section selected was one of the most dramatic in the poem). Pupils were invited to comment on both the reading and the freeze-frame, and in so doing drew not just on the criteria but also on their interpretation of the poem. In this way, the dual nature of the lesson – developing their understanding of the literature and of speaking and listening – was also served.

P: It [the performance] was boring.
T: What do you mean, 'boring'?
P: There wasn't enough expression in your face when the poem was being read or in the reading.
T: So what could I have done to make it better?
P: You could have looked and sounded more alarmed.
T: Like this? [strikes a pose]
P: Not quite.
T: More like this? [strikes another pose]
P: Yeah.

Discussion between pupils

If we now turn our attention to the discussion that occurs between the pupils when they are engaged in the task and in peer assessment we again see how the activities were initially framed contributes to the quality of pupil discussion. In lesson A, the correcting of the text was undertaken in almost complete silence, as was the peer assessment. The way in which the scope of the peer assessment had been defined by the previous task – largely a proofreading exercise – meant that there was no opportunity for them to discuss what they thought of the letters or how they might be improved, other than in terms of spelling, punctuation and grammar.

Pupils in lesson B, on the other hand, were involved in a lively, extended discussion, first on how to render dramatically their section of the poem and then in critiquing the performance of their peers. In so doing they too built on their understanding of the scope of the task as established by the previous activities. Each performance was the result of collaboration between the pupils in which, as they had done in the previous two activities, they extended their own understanding through the contributions and ideas of their peers. That they understood the task of performing the poem to be open-ended was evident in the wide variety of interpretations. That they understood how to make judgements as to quality in order to improve performance was demonstrated through the comments they made to their peers.

Conclusion

What is evident in these two lessons is that the quality of classroom talk – the questions the teacher can ask and the dialogue in which pupils can engage – cannot be isolated from the activities undertaken in the lesson. As we observed in the section on principles of learning, the richer the task the greater the opportunity to extend and develop pupils' thinking through talk. This idea is examined further in the section on feedback.

6. Feedback

Oral feedback

Much of the feedback that teachers give is oral. Again, the formative quality and effectiveness of that feedback depends on the task. The snippets of dialogue below come from a Year 11 lesson in which the class was studying the Carol-Anne Duffy poem 'Before You Were Mine'. The poem has a complex point of view, in which Duffy speculates about her mother before she, Carol-Anne Duffy, was born. For homework, the teacher had asked the pupils to interview their parents about their lives before they had children, and the first activity was to get the pupils to share with each other what they had found out. Only after they did this did they look at the poem. The teacher, Catherine, explained that Duffy was, in effect, asking her mother the same sort of questions they had asked their parents. She then asked them, in pairs, to explore the poem by suggesting that they consider what kind of questions they would like to ask Duffy herself. The following dialogue was the result. For the purposes of this section, however, we have concentrated on the teachers' interventions because we wish to examine the nature of the feedback she is giving.

Pair 1

'What do you think?' [Pupil responds]
'She could be.' [Pupil responds]
'Right, that's what I mean by unusual perspective. You don't really write about something before you were born.'
'Don't get hung up on the first line.'

Pair 2

'Any other reasons why she's comparing her mother to Marilyn?' [Pupil responds]
'Anything else? Think about her representation.' [Another pupil responds]
'Think about how her public viewed her.' [Teacher pauses, then prompts] 'She's famous.'
'So why compare her with her mother?' [Pupils respond and are led to idea that she's an 'icon of the age']

Pair 3

'You're raising a question, aren't you? Write that down as your first question.'
'No, there are no answers. Perhaps the group will help you.'
'How will you phrase it? Is that what you mean?'

Pair 4

A boy talks at length and the teacher responds, 'How?' The pupil continues his train of thought and the teacher ends the exchange by saying 'I think you might be reading too much into it.'

Pair 5

'Not much annotation going on.' She then listens again and adds, 'You want to look at this one', before moving on.

Pair 6

'What's the comparison that's being set up?'
'Good question. Is it?'
'We don't usually think…'
'Why does she say…? What's the point of the simile?' [Pupil responds]
'I mean, if you think about it, the five senses.'
'I mean, do you not associate people with scent?' [Pupil responds]
'So, an unusual simile.'

Pair 7

'Is this what…? That could be one of your questions.'
'I'm not going to tell you what to think.' [Pupil responds]
'Yes, that's exactly what she's saying – that's why it's a good question to ask.'

Pair 8

[Looks over their shoulders]
'That's very interesting. Any other connotations with that word?' [This prompts several responses]

What should be noted first is that Catherine's planning and interventions suggest that she knows her pupils well, which is important if she is to provide meaningful, formative feedback. She can plan a lesson that will engage and challenge them and she can see at a glance who needs to be cajoled and who can be left alone. Without prior knowledge of their attainment and working patterns it is unlikely that she would be able to make these judgements as quickly and effectively as she does.

The teacher has also created sufficient trust within the class that she is able to tell pupils, as in pairs 1 and 4, that they are going in the wrong direction, without undermining their confidence. In fact, these two pairs both went on to produce insightful comments on the poem, which suggests that the pupils trust her judgement and are willing to listen to her.

How pupils come to trust teachers in this way is a complex process, but an important element is that Catherine's interventions suggest to the pupils that she is genuinely listening and interested in what they have to say, rather than simply telling them what to think. Her interventions are all focused on the task of improving the pupils' work rather than on judging them, and they can see how her questions are designed to make them think further. In this way the dialogue in her classroom has the flavour of what might be called authentic conversation, as opposed to the ritualised ping-pong match of so much classroom exchange. Indeed, one feature of effective teacher–student talk is that one can imagine the same sort of dialogue occurring outside an educational setting, which is rarely the case with traditional teacher–pupil exchanges.

And it is this that gives the interventions their formative flavour. For what is interesting about the interventions is that they vary considerably; all are impromptu and differentiated, each constituting a response to the pupils' thinking. For example, Catherine is considerably more directive with some pairs than with others, suggesting that she believes some pupils need more guidance and structure. These range from the demand that the pupils actually get on with the work, as in pair 5, through closely structured exchanges, as with pairs 2 and 6, to the more open prompts in pair 8.

These exchanges also illuminate subject-specific issues; for Catherine's discussion with the pupils highlights a tension within English teaching between a desire for openness and originality of response on the part of the pupils, as against appreciating a more received or conventional understanding of a text or concept. There is, however, a fine line between over- and under-direction, by the teacher, within that tension.

In a sense, maintaining that very fine line is part of the skill of the good teacher and is dependent on his/her own subject knowledge, assessment of the pupils' responses and the subsequent feedback. Interestingly, Catherine steers them away from certain avenues of interpretation: 'Don't get hung up on the first line'; 'I think you might be reading too much into it' (pairs 1 and 4), while at the same time encouraging open responses, as with pairs 7 and 8. As we have already noted, pairs 1 and 4 were helped by this intervention.

Written feedback

Not all feedback is, however, oral; some is written. There are, however, difficulties in discussing this element in isolation from the next section, 'Sharing success criteria with the learner', not only because helpful written feedback should relate to the way in which the teacher has made the aims of the task explicit but also because writing appropriate comments to develop a pupil's work is sometimes challenging.

Planning for feedback

So perhaps the most important principle to note is that comments are considerably less effective unless time is set aside for pupils to act upon them. Many of the comments we write are often what might be called 'micro-summative'. In other words they allow the pupil no opportunity to use the feedback to alter what they have done in the lesson but simply sum up the performance they have just completed. Furthermore, comments made at the end of a unit of work generally relate only to the work just undertaken and have little relevance, other than technical concerns, to the next unit. Except for surface comments, such as spelling, punctuation and grammar, feedback that might be relevant to a scheme on ballads is unlikely to be immediately helpful in media analysis.

For this reason, therefore, the drafting stage of a piece of work is possibly the most appropriate time for extensive written comments, designed to aid progress, to be made. We will consider the pupils' role in this process in the section on peer and self-assessment, but for now it is worth noting that, as with oral feedback, some of the best written feedback is dialogic. Marginal or numbered notes which prompt the pupils to think further and question what they have written are key ways in which teachers can be formative in their comments. Even simple observations such as 'Why do you think this?', 'Could you explain this further?', 'What about…?', 'Tell me more about…' and 'I need more description to help me understand this' all encourage the development of ideas. Identifying what the pupil might build on is also helpful: 'I like the way you have created a spooky feel here', 'That's a very good point – well supported', even a 'yes' in the text can confirm a good argument or significant moment in a story.

Because of the powerful role that comments can make in improving quality it is important to identify which pieces of work will need extended written feedback and, also, to build in the opportunity for redrafting into any scheme of work. Not all work, however, needs redrafting or extensive comments; much of the work in class is a preparatory staging post towards the first draft and then to the final copy, and all that is needed is checking for completion. Nevertheless, these more minor, contributory pieces of work provide important opportunities for teachers to glean the extent to which pupils are engaging with the scheme or need supplementary help. Many English teachers in the project began to find it useful, therefore, to build slack into any scheme of work in order to provide additional time for a class if the need arose.

Feedback on accuracy and quality

On the surface, comments on technical accuracy appear easier to make. They have the apparent advantage of seeming concrete and about certainties – rightness and wrongness. They are also generic and, as we observed earlier, this means that they seem appropriate to set as targets. Actually engaging pupils in technical errors through

effective feedback is, however, more complex and the same principles, outlined above, about giving pupils time to engage with technical feedback, pertain. As the research reviewed in Black and Wiliam (1998b) makes clear, such feedback rarely has any impact on learning because there is nothing left for the pupil to do. Some teachers require students to copy out spelling mistakes, but this is equally unsuccessful since there is no requirement for the students to think. Again, some of these will be considered in peer and self-assessment.

Having said this, pupils do need to master the conventions of English and, as the publications of the English and Media Centre (no date) or the National Writing Project make clear, this is best taught in the context of pupils' own work. For example, instead of marking everything, the teacher can:

- provide feedback on a specific aspect of the pupil's work;
- identify particular patterns of error in pupils' work;
- provide 'scaffolded' feedback, such as placing a dot in the margin for each error, and requiring the student to find the errors and fix them;
- refer pupils to morphological or etymological patterns in spelling and help them identify these in their work;
- provide pupils with the opportunity to

read their work aloud as a way of identifying points for punctuation.

Issues of quality are, by their nature, more difficult to grapple with; not only because the scope of such feedback is so much greater, which is why, of course, it is so important in developing pupil achievement in English, but also, more fundamentally, because it is so hard to define. On the surface it covers two broad areas – content and style: what you are trying to say and how you say it. Again, the former has always been easier to write feedback on because it appears to have the advantage of being more concrete. As we discussed earlier in this section, the best written feedback on the content of work is feedback that promotes further thinking and will, therefore, often be in the form of a question or a statement that implies a specific action – 'Is there any evidence of this?', 'quote'.

But these two elements are not unrelated. One of the most important ways in which a teacher can help pupils with their written work is to enable them to position themselves as a reader when writing. In other words, they need to think in terms of their audience, not just in terms of altering the genre in which they write for a specific audience, but to understand that writing is in essence about communicating with a reader. Comments that facilitate this tend to merge consideration of style and content, for example 'I need you to tell me more about what he looked like'; 'How did this make her feel?'; 'I'm not clear what you are trying to say here'; 'How else might you put that?'. Or positively – 'Yes, I see what you mean'; 'You've put that really well'. In this way feedback becomes an engaged dialogue between the reader and the writer in an effort to improve communication.

7. Sharing success criteria with the learner

An undercurrent to the discussion so far has been the fact that quality in English is an elusive property, so that ensuring that pupils come to understand the success criteria against which their work will be judged, while essential, is problematic. Much recent attention has been given to two main approaches to circumvent this problem – genre studies and grammar for writing. A full discussion on these two methods can be found in the NATE booklet *English Assessed* (Marshall 2004a), but here we will take a slightly different tack. This is because while both approaches have much to commend them, they can oversimplify the complexity of a good piece of writing or speech and so misrepresent for the pupil what needs to be done (see section 4, 'Principles of learning').

Moreover, they can overemphasise the rule or formula at the expense of meaning. In these circumstances performance can become about demonstrating adherence to a predetermined form or formula rather than the ideas or narrative to be told. And as Dewey (1907) observed, 'There is all the difference in the world between having to say something and having something to say' (p.67). The model of English we are exemplifying below, then, is English as a language art.

Instead, as we noted in the section on the principles of learning, this booklet will concentrate on the notion of apprenticing pupils into the guild knowledge – shared by teachers about what it means to be good at English – as the chief lever of progression and formative practice (Sadler 1989). Clearly, peer assessment is one of the main vehicles by which pupils will engage in issues of quality in their own writing and we will discuss this in the next section of this booklet. Another key way in which teachers share the criteria is through modelling good practice. As with all other discussion in this booklet the main aim is to help pupils understand for themselves what they need to do to improve. Activities need therefore to be designed to help pupils think about these issues instead of memorising a formula. As with previous sections, planning is a vital part of this formative process. We will look at two examples to illustrate how this might be achieved.

Modelling quality through the progression of activities

If we return to the lesson we considered at the start of the booklet on pre-twentieth-century poetry, we see how each stage of the lesson draws the pupils further into engaging with issues as to what makes for a quality performance.

Year 8 lesson B: Pre-twentieth-century poem
- Class draw up a list of criteria guided by teacher.
- Teacher and LSA perform the poem.
- Pupils asked to critique the performance.
- Pupils rehearse the performance.
- Pupils peer-assess poems based on criteria.
- Pupils perform poems based on criteria.

Pupils in this lesson engaged in both technical considerations, such as clarity and accuracy, and the higher order, interpretive concepts of meaning and effect. Crucially, however, it was the sequence of activities which guided the pupils towards deepening their understanding and so becoming independent. This is because the tasks, including encouraging the pupils to create their own criteria, helped them to think for themselves about what might be needed to capture the meaning of the poem in performance and asked them to apply this understanding.

Each stage of the lesson offered pupils an opportunity to refine and test that understanding of what was required through criticism and creative activity – both significant skills in English. In this way the pupils in lesson B began to engage in the more complex issues of any performance in English, be it verbal or written. In other words, the pupils were asked to engage in the relationship between the meaning of a product and the way in which that meaning is expressed – between the form and the content.

If we now look at another lesson sequence we see how the teacher actively engages the pupils in the reader–writer relationship as a way of helping them engage in the notion of quality.

Year 7 lesson – autobiography

Lesson 1

- Teacher handed out minimalist version of a story called 'The Sick Boy'.
- Pupils invited to annotate text, in pairs, with questions about what they would like to know more about.
- Questions collated on the board.
- Extract from Laurie Lee's *Cider with Rosie* given out in which he describes an incident in which he nearly died.
- Pupils invited to discover whether their questions were answered in the text by answering them.

Lesson 2

- Pupils asked to discuss which questions elicited more interesting information and these were scribed on the board.
- From this, pupils were asked to draw up a list of criteria for writing autobiographies.
- Pupils began the first draft of their own autobiography using the criteria (pupils used criteria in subsequent lessons to peer-assess).

Most importantly, again, the tasks are designed to involve the pupils in thinking about what makes a good piece of writing. Inherent within the first activity is an attempt to begin to help pupils understand and articulate their own criteria for quality. This is then refined and developed through the subsequent, carefully and incrementally scaffolded activities. Yet what is significant about each of the activities is that the whole thrust of the lessons is on the pupils' active involvement in their own learning and knowledge creation. The tasks demanded that the pupils did the thinking.

The initial task, in effect, enables pupils to create their own comprehension exercise which foregrounds the issue of the craft of the writer in making a text interesting to the reader. Answering their own questions allows them to identify where, and thus exemplify how, Laurie Lee satisfies the criteria that they, as a class, have established for what would interest them in a piece of writing. From this they are able to create a specific template or framework for good autobiographical writing, which they could then use in their own work. This same framework also enabled the pupils to reflect on the quality of their own autobiographies and to provide effective feedback, using criteria mutually understood, when assessing the work of their peers.

But these lessons, as we first observed, are also enabling pupils to develop their own skills as writers through a deepening understanding of the reader–writer relationship: a growing knowledge of the craft of writing and the ability of authors to shape meaning, experience and ideas to have an impact on the reader. For this teacher, such development occurs in the pupils by encouraging both their critical and creative faculties in their capacities as consumers and producers of the printed word. It is about English as a language art.

In this instance she draws on the pupils' own life experiences, either as readers or through empathy, as a way of enabling them to identify with the characters. Next she guides them to abstract that understanding and use it to help them consider the reader–writer relationship as a means of improving their own writing. Throughout, she is helping them to learn how to position themselves as readers when they are writing by making them

aware of what they want from an author when reading.

Conclusion

Both these are quite formal examples of how this might be achieved, but simpler discussions can start useful trains of thought. Starting a scheme on horror writing, for example by asking pupils what frightens them, is a more informal way of achieving a similar end. Each of the lessons examined above, however, illustrates ways in which pupils can be encouraged through structured, carefully sequenced activities to engage with questions of quality, both critically and creatively. They show how pupils can be asked to work through their ideas on what makes for a quality performance, apply that understanding and further refine it through peer assessment. In this way, sharing the criteria with the learners becomes less about teachers stating objectives on the board and more about pupils being apprenticed into the guild.

8. Peer and self-assessment

Peer and self-assessment is, however, vital to this process. The potency of peer and self-assessment in improving achievement in English has long been recognised. Peer assessment was strongly advocated, for example, in the National Writing Project publications as an opportunity for pupils to learn from each other. As we outlined in the section on principles of learning, a collaborative model by which pupils discuss their work – both the ideas and text – with writing partners is an important aid to progression. Reading the work of their peers provides pupils with a similar kind of opportunity to that which teachers have in standardisation meetings. It helps them, through exemplification, to engage with what work at a particular level or grade looks like (the 'construct') and also enables them to see how a piece of work might be approached, and so understand issues of quality (see section 4).

In this way peer assessment is one of the main vehicles to promote self-assessment. Seeing how someone else has tackled the same assignment helps pupils reflect on their own performance. For this reason it is fairly common practice in English and has been one of the main starting points of the English teachers, with whom we have worked, for adopting formative strategies in their classrooms. They became more systematic, however, and less ad hoc in the way in which they engaged pupils in peer assessment as a means of enhancing its impact.

Part of this involved, as we have already discussed, planning for peer assessment in a scheme of work; but it also entailed having all the other elements considered in this booklet in place. If we look at the peer comments on the piece of Year 10 coursework below, the point becomes clearer. The teacher stuck the essay onto the centre of an A3 sheet of paper and asked the pupils to annotate/comment on the text on either side. The work was a diary entry by Romeo.

The sophistication of this pupil's comments on a peer's work exemplifies much that we have looked at when considering quality feedback. The commentator identifies specific things that the pupil has done well (points 4, 7, 8 and 9) and the comments helpfully blend ideas on both the content and the way in which it is expressed, including relating punctuation to meaning (point 1). But such quality does not come without several other factors being in place.

To begin with, the teacher has created a safe environment in which pupils feel comfortable having others read their work. Collaboration and the sharing of practice have become the norm. Some teachers encourage this by allowing their own performance to be critiqued, as in the example of the Year 8 pre-twentieth-century poetry lesson discussed earlier. It is clear, too, that the class teacher has modelled good feedback herself, both in the way she has talked with the class and through her own written comments. And, as with everything else, pupils need to see examples of good practice to be able to know what to do. The pupil's own understanding of the text is also evident in the comments. This does not occur without giving pupils time to think and talk about the play.

Year 10 example of peer assessment (points not numbered in original)	
1. Lots of points blended together. It gets confusing without any [sic]	6. Too brief – 'Mercutio wants to fight'… 'then they were fighting'. You need more info and emotions in between what causes them to fight – do they threaten each other first?
2. This sentence doesn't work well. You can't use two becauses in a sentence. Too many ands.	7. Good explanations and emotions.
3. A bit vague. Mercutio doesn't just die; he suffered. Maybe add some quotes from Mercutio.	8. Good thoughts and opinions from Romeo on the situation.
4. Good choise [sic] of words. They are good to describe Romeo's feelings.	9. I like this bit when he says 'it was over'. You could maybe add finally info to describe how glad he is for it to be over.
5. More descriptive bits for Tybalt's death, not just he fell over dead.	10. Lots of good points. Everything is included. Try to space out all of the events instead of blending them all together. This makes it a bit confusing to read. Second half a lot better than the first half.

Finally, through the comments, it is possible to see how this pupil has engaged with the complexity and layering of criteria in this assignment, showing an understanding of what makes for a quality piece of work. These include the need for quotation (3), description (5), vocabulary (4), clarity (3) avoiding, on this occasion, repetition (2), empathy (3 and 6), explanation (7), imaginative engagement (8 and 9), coherent structure (10) – the list could go on. Any oversimplification of the criteria (see Sadler 1989) would have diminished the quality of this response. The pupil who received the comments would have been in little doubt about what he/she did well and what he/she needed to do to improve.

In a way this exercise exemplifies part of what we are aiming to do as English teachers – to enable pupils to reflect on their own and others' work and to use their critical faculties to improve their creativity.

9. Sharing good practice

The ideas in this booklet are intended as a starting point for those who are interested in improving their practice, but we have to admit that not one of the ideas that we have discussed in this booklet is new. What is new is the evidence that attention to these processes, for so long at the heart of shared definitions of what constitutes good practice in the teaching of English, is one of the ways, possibly the most powerful way, of raising student achievement. What is also new is that we are beginning to discover that understanding what we want to change about our practice is only a starting point. The hard part is consistently enacting these ideas in our practice. The work we have done with teachers suggests that the teachers who are most successful are those who change their practice slowly, by focusing on only two or three aspects at a time. As they become skilled with these new ideas, and incorporate them into their natural practice, they can then turn their attention to new ideas. Teachers who try to change many things about their practice at the same time are unlikely to be successful.

The other thing that appears to be crucial, if teachers are to develop their practice in fruitful ways, is support. We know of a small number of examples where teachers have managed to implement radical changes in their practice on their own, but these are rare. Successful development of our practice is far more likely if we can draw on the support of our peers, and two forms of support have, in our experience, been particularly important.

The first is to meet regularly – ideally once a month – with other teachers who are trying to make similar changes in their practice. Many teachers have told us that it was the fact that they were going to have to talk to their colleagues about their experiences in trying these ideas out that forced them to try them in their classroom. The second is to arrange for a trusted peer to observe our teaching, and provide feedback. The crucial feature of such peer observations is that the agenda for the observation must be set by the teacher being observed. Additionally, where the teacher being observed tells the peer not only what to look for but also what would count, for the teacher being observed, as evidence of success or failure, there is less chance of the observer introducing his/her own biases and prejudices into the process.

With these elements – practical ways for taking small steps in developing one's practice, and support from one's colleagues – formative assessment can produce substantial and sustained improvements in student achievement and make teaching more enjoyable and rewarding professionally.

References

Barnes, D., Britton, J. and Torbe, M. (1972) *Language, the Learner and the School*. London: Penguin.

Barrs, M. (2003) *Writing through Reading*. London: Centre for Primary Language.

Black, P., Harrison, C., Lee, C., Marshall, B. and Wiliam, D. (2002) *Working Inside the Black Box: Assessment for Learning in the Classroom*. London: nferNelson.

Black, P., Harrison, C., Lee, C., Marshall, B. and Wiliam, D. (2003) *Assessment for Learning: Putting It into Practice*. Buckingham: Open University Press.

Black, P. and Wiliam, D. (1998a) *Inside the Black Box: Raising Standards through Classroom Assessment*. London: King's College London School of Education.

Black, P. and Wiliam, D. (1998b) 'Assessment and classroom learning'. *Assessment in Education: Principles, Policy and Practice*, 5(1), 7–73.

Carter, R. (ed.) (1992) *Language in the National Curriculum: Materials for Professional Development*. Nottingham: Nottingham University Department of English.

Corden, R. (2000) *Literacy and Learning through Talk: Strategies for the Primary Classroom*. Buckingham: Open University Press.

DES and WO (1990a) *A Report of the Committee of Inquiry into the Teaching of English* [The Kingman Report]. London: HMSO.

DES and WO (1990b) *English in the National Curriculum (no. 2)*. London: HMSO.

Dewey, J. (1907) *The School and Society*. Chicago, IL: University of Chicago Press.

DFE and WO (1995) *English in the National Curriculum*. London: HMSO.

DfEE (1998) *The National Literacy Strategy: Framework for Teaching* (Vol. PP3/31981/298/124). London: HMSO.

DfEE (2001) *The National Literacy Strategy: Framework for Teaching English: Years 7, 8 & 9* (Vol. 0019/2001). London: DfEE.

DfEE/QCA (2000) *English: The National Curriculum Handbook for Primary Teachers in England: Key Stages 1 & 2*. London: HMSO.

DfEE/QCA (2000) *The National Curriculum Handbook for Secondary Teachers in England: Key Stages 3 & 4*. London: HMSO.

English and Media Centre (n.d.) *English Curriculum: Writing: Materials for Discussion*. London: English and Media Centre.

Howse, C. (2004) *Daily Telegraph*, 26 October.

Marshall, B. (2000) *English Teachers: The Unofficial Guide: Researching the Philosophies of English Teachers*. London: RoutledgeFalmer.

Marshall, B. (2004a) *English Assessed: Formative Assessment in English.* Sheffield: NATE.

Marshall, B. (2004b) 'Goals or horizons: the conundrum of progression in English, or a possible way of understanding formative assessment in English'. *The Curriculum Journal,* 15(2), 101–13.

Morgan, W. and Wyatt-Smith, C. M. (2000) 'Improper accountability: towards a theory of critical literacy'. *Assessment in Education: Principles, Policy and Practice* 7(1), 123–42.

Perrenoud, P. (1998) 'From formative evaluation to a controlled regulation of learning processes: towards a wider conceptual field'. *Assessment in Education: Principles, Policy and Practice,* 5(1), 85–102.

Sadler, D. R. (1989) 'Formative assessment and the design of instructional systems'. *Instructional Science,* 18, 119–44.

Wiliam, D. (2000) 'The meanings and consequences of educational assessments'. *Critical Quarterly,* 42(1), 105–27.

Wiliam, D., Lee, C., Harrison, C. and Black, P. (2004) 'Teachers developing assessment for learning: impact on student achievement'. *Assessment in Education: Principles, Policy and Practice,* 11(1), 49–65.

Useful websites

Assessment Reform Group: arg.educ.cam.ac.uk

Association for Achievement and Improvement through Assessment (AAIR): www.aaia.org.uk

Department for Education and Skills (DfES): www.standards.dfes.gov.uk

General Teaching Council www.gtce.org.uk/research

Qualifications and Curriculum Authority (QCA): www.qca.org.uk

King's College Assessment for Learning Group: www.kcl.ac.uk/education/research/kal.html